BE GOOD TO YOUR MONEY

And Your Money Will Be Good To You!

BE GOOD TO YOUR MONEY

AND YOUR MONEY WILL BE GOOD TO YOU!

Lisa Frye

Foreword by Quentin R. Sampson

L L Q PUBLISHING

To my son, Quintin, for all that you have taught me.

****

To my first financial wizards, my mother and grandmother (your memories live on).

When I look into the future, it's so bright it
burns my eyes.   Oprah Winfrey

Surround yourself with only people who are
going to lift you higher.   Oprah Winfrey

About the Author

Lisa Frye is an insurance broker, real estate agent, and a real estate investor. She is the owner of several businesses, including an elementary school.

In 1999, she received the Thomas Jefferson Award from NBC5 Chicago for her community service, which includes being a member of several Boards.

She is the past Youth Chairperson of the Chicago South Chapter of NAIC, and past Coach of the Millennium Millionaires Youth Model Investment Club.

She has been featured on the *Thomas Jefferson Award* program, *Where In The World Is Art?*, *Thread The Needle,* and in *Young Money Matters.*

But most importantly, she is a mother to her teenage son, Quintin, who is, also, an entrepreneur and investor.

Build a better mousetrap and the world will
beat a path to your door.   Ralph Waldo
                    Emerson

Hitch your wagon to a star.

                                    Ralph Waldo Emerson

Quentin R. Sampson

Director, National Investors Association

Chairperson, Chicago South Chapter of NAIC

In 1992, after 35 years of employment, I retired from Peoples Gas Light and Coke Company (a subsidiary of Peoples Energy). Before retirement, I participated in my company's stock purchase discount program. The company's stock flourished. I made money, and it felt good. So, I decided to invest in other stocks, without using any investment strategies, just my very limited knowledge of investing. I was what they call a "noise investor"-someone who chases the latest *hot* stock in the media. Boy, was that a big mistake, for I lost my money! This is not an effective strategy for adding value to your portfolio.

In an effort to educate myself about investing and investing in the stock market, I came across the National Association of Investors Corporation (NAIC). I became involved with the NAIC and applied their strategies to guide me in my investment decisions. Through wise money management, I have been able to provide a very comfortable lifestyle and retirement for myself and my family.

Both new and experienced investors can benefit from the strategies of NAIC (a nonprofit educational group). I will share with you some of the investment strategies that I have learned through my involvement with NAIC.

1. Invest in Growth Companies-Growth companies can be defined as those companies that have outperformed their competitors by producing better than average gains in earnings. Over the long run, growth stocks tend to appreciate more in value than slower-growing stocks.

2. Set Investment Objectives-NAIC recommends that you should consider setting your investment goals to double your money every five years, which is a compound annual growth rate of 14.9%.

3. Do Your Research-You should never purchase a stock without some formal analysis. Do your *own* homework, research your investments using a variety of sources, such as Value Line, Standard & Poor's stock fact sheets (both can be found at your local library) or use online resources on the Internet.

4. <u>Consider Low Cost Investing Methods</u>-
   Investors starting out small should focus on
   keeping the cost of investing down. Unique
   choices for low cost investing includes:
   making use of Dividend Reinvestment Plans
   (DRIPS's), companies with Direct Purchase
   Plans, discount brokerage firms, or
   participation in an investment club.

5. <u>Make Use of Dollar Cost Averaging</u>-When
   you make consistent stock purchases with a
   regular sum of money, regardless of the
   market's level or a specific stock price at
   that moment, you are making use of dollar
   cost averaging. As the market is rising over
   time, you'll buy more shares when the stock
   price is low and fewer shares when they are
   high, but your average overall cost of
   purchasing shares will be lower over time.

6. <u>Diversify Your Holdings</u>-Diversification is an
   important way to reduce investing risk and
   increasing your investing opportunity. As an
   investor, this means buying stocks in a
   range of different industries and of differing
   size: small, medium, and large companies.

7. <u>Review Your Stocks Periodically</u>-Many
   investors think that the biggest challenge is
   making a sound decision when purchasing a
   stock initially. The error lies in not managing

the stock once it has been purchased. Successful investors review their portfolio periodically to ensure that the stock is meeting the goals originally indicated when it was purchased.

8. When Investing, Be Patient-Stock prices fluctuate. Even though downward trends can last for a while, the overall movement in the stock market has been upward, at about 9% compounded annually since 1900. An investor's best strategy is to purchase companies with good fundamentals at a reasonable price.

For a free NAIC Investor's Kit, contact NAIC at:

NAIC, 711 West 13 Mile Road, Madison Heights, MI 48071. Call toll free-1-877-ASK-NAIC (275-6242) or visit their website at: www.better-investing.org.

As you move toward becoming better money managers, being good to your money is an important start. There are many benefits in being good to your money. As you reap the benefits, you will be able to say that your money has been good to you.

Introduction

Facing the true reason why we are having money problems hurt, and we know it. To face the truth, *instant gratification* has gotten most of us in overwhelming debt and is the number one reason for financial disaster. The urge to have it RIGHT NOW can be very overpowering. It is the urge that can take you from $0 to $100,000 in debt in minutes. It is the urge that will cause you to buy the 5th pair of red shoes. It is the urge that will make you buy the latest electronic device at an unbelievable price (not remembering, that you never learned how to operate the last one). It is the urge that makes you sign up for a trip to the Bahamas with the mortgage payment (and you think gamblers have a problem). It is the urge that has made you time and time again do things, with money, that you realize you should not do.

During my lifetime, I have met some very wealthy people, many of them self-made millionaires. One of the factors that they contributes to their success is their money consciousness. They know how to control their spending habits, how to shop around for the best deal, how to recognize the value of the dollar, and how important it is to save as much as possible. They do not waste their money on lavish lifestyles. Their ultimate goal is to save from their earnings, and to save when spending. Now, they are living comfortable lives with a secure future.

This book will cover various areas of your life, and provide insight into living like a millionaire, without being a millionaire. If you have a shortage of money, this book will show you areas of your life that may be very costly to you.

At this point, many of you will not have millionaire status, but if you are consistent in applying everything that you will learn, you will arrive into the millionaire status. I have used all of these strategies, many times over. I have shared them with family and friends. Now, I'm going to share them with you. This book will, also, share with you some of the consumer strategies that I have learned over the years, after becoming more conscience of my spending habits. I will show you how to reduce your cost of living without decreasing your standard of living (unless, your standard of living is determined by the Jones).

My two caregivers, mom and dad, died when I was 13 and 18, respectively. In dealing with the grief, I became the queen of instant gratification. I had to have whatever I wanted sooner than now. So, I quickly maxed-out 15 credit credits. Plus, I had an American Express, Diner's Club, and Carte Blanche card to cover any declines.

Becoming a single-parent caused me to look at money differently. I had to begin to think of others and not just myself. Before, I never had a second thought about buying the BEST. I remember in the 70's, I had a top brand-name house slipper in every color they made-at a cost of $25 a pair. I, also, bought robes (at $45 each) to match the house slippers. My robes and house slippers cost me over $700. That was a costly lesson and costly dressing for a high schooler.

There are certain principles that operate regarding money. These principles have been shown throughout time. These principles govern how we **receive** money. If you handle your money poorly, you will never have enough. That is, if you are burdened with debt, throwing away your money on frills and thrills, spending above and beyond your means, paying high interest rates and late fees, and having no financial goals, your money will take off. *It will leave you.* It will go to other sources that draw it. On the other hand, if you manage your money, *more money* will come your way. If you are saving, investing, and budgeting your money, you will cause money to run to you in the form of additional income, interest, dividends, and capital gain. You will **receive** the money that poor money managers have thrown away.

I hope that you will use the tools in this book to avoid problems. I hope that you will use it to avoid debt. It's easier to avoid a problem than to solve it later. It's easier to stay out of debt, than it is to get out of debt.

I'm sure that you have heard the phrase "money attracts money". You must have money to attract other money. How do you get the money? Learn to manage the money that you have, regardless of how little. The little will become a lot. A lot will attract more and more money. It is not about the amount of money you have, but what you do with the money and how much you keep.

My friends call me "cheap". I accept the title and *wear* it well. However, my self-gratification is being able to sit down on the first of the month and pay *all* of my bills for the month. My self-gratification is paying all of my bills for the month with money left over to invest and to give to charity. My self-gratification is having savings accounts, money market accounts, retirement funds, CD s, a stock portfolio, and investment properties. Being financially blessed is such a *great* feeling!!

The strategies in this book have changed my life completely. Over the years, I have been able to save thousands of dollars, and so have my family and friends. Some are having the same financial success that I am having. Some are still waiting on the Prize Patrol and/or the Lottery. Please use this book to create your own financial success. For, I wish you the same financial success. Start now and.......

Be good to your money and your money will be good to you!

Lisa Frye

Take therefore the talent (or money) from him, and give it unto him which hath ten talents. For unto every one that hath shall be given, and he shall have abundance; but from him that hath not shall be taken away even that which he hath. And cast ye the unprofitable servant into outer darkness.

Matthew 25: 28-30

CONTENTS

Aim for the moon. If you miss, you may hit a
star.

W. Clement Stone

1

GOALS

It is important to have goals for every aspect of your life-personal and professional. It is very important to have financial goals. Without the proper finances, many goals are unattainable.

Here, we will deal with setting financial goals for yourself and your family. We will discuss financial goals for your kids in Chapter 9.

Long before I understood how effective and important goals were in my life, I had goals. In elementary school, I had goals for being on the honor roll. In junior high, I had goals for going to college. During high school, I redefined those goals and determined which college I wanted to attend and my career interest. To me, obtaining those goals meant fulfilling my life expectations.

It is important to *always* have goals that you are trying to obtain. At any one time, I have two or three goals that I am attempting to accomplish. Words can't describe my sense of accomplishment, as I attain each goal. As each goal is attained, there is always another goal waiting in the wind to take its place in my life.

It is most important to write down your goals. You will need to revisit them from time to time. They will become the road map you will need to follow to get you from one destination to the next.

Your personal goals may include buying a car, going to college, going back to college, taking a vacation, or going to a concert.

Your financial goals should consist of long-term and short-term goals. Long term goals are the things that you plan for later in your life or in approximately 5 years or more, such as college, buying a house, starting a business, or retirement. For long-term goals, it helps to put money aside and determine how best to invest it. That way, your money will be working for you, through interest, capital gains, and/or dividends, while you wait to use it.

Short-term goals are the things that you will

need money for in the near future. Short-term goals may include such things as buying Christmas gifts, going to a concert, going to a spa, or saving for a rainy day.

Both of these goals should be continuous. Once you buy that lovely living room sofa, that doesn't mean that you should stop funding that account. Goals are continuous, so should the account that funds the goals.

Develop your financial goals by using the form on the next page. Feel free to copy the form, as your goals will continue to change. As you accomplish each goal, cross it off of your list. When you accomplish at least three goals in each category, re-do your list. Do not destroy your old list, as it will be important in evaluating your financial success. At the end of the year, look over your old lists and see how much you have advanced financially. Compare your yesterdays to your today.

Obstacles don't have to stop you. If you run into a wall, don't turn around and give up. Figure out how to climb it, go through it, or work around it.   *Michael Jordan*

LONG TERM GOALS

Date_____

1._____

2._____

3._____

4._____

5._____

6._____

SHORT TERM GOALS

Date_____

1._____

2._____

3._____

4._____

5._____

6._____

BUDGETING

To be able to determine how much money you will be able to allocate toward your goals, you will need to create a budget. A budget, along with consistency, are key to your financial success.

Write down your goals, then make a budget. Your budget should be as simple as possible. If not, you will not be motivated to keep it up.

Your budget should include how much you earn and how much your necessities cost. Necessities include housing, utilities, insurance, food, car payments, medical expenses, and savings. You should do two budgets: annual and monthly.

Creating a budget takes the cooperation of *every* family member. Many times, the adults are the ones that create the budget. Kids are people, too, and they spend monies that are included in the budget. It is important that the kids are included, so they can begin to understand that money does not grow in the ATM machine. Plus, you can help them do a budget for themselves. And, they will have an understanding of what you can and can not do, financially.

Many times, parents are rebutant to do a budget with the kids. They don't want the kids to know or see that the liabilities exceed the assets, that is, that the bills exceed the income. They are too embarrassed to sit down and expose themselves. If you are guilty of feeling this way, then you need a serious financial check-up and NOW!

Budgeting is the best way to determine where your money is going. Are you wasting your money or spending it wisely? Are you being good to your money?

The main purpose of a budget is to help you control your money. You always want to know how much money is coming in and how much money is going out. You always want to have more money saved than you need to spend.

The main categories of your budget are:

Housing

Food

Transportation

Clothing

Insurance and medical expenses

Entertainment and recreation

Savings (long and short term)

Miscellaneous

Each of these areas will be discussed in more details in the following chapters.

Many people have asked how much is too much and how much is too little to allocate for each category in your budget. The amount will vary based on the number of members in your family, your family needs, and your income. Here are the guidelines that you can use to get started (I, also, use them). The amounts are calculated from your net income.

Housing   **25 to 30%**

Household goods   **15 to 20%**

Transportation   **10 to 15%**

Clothing   **4 to 5%**

Insurance/Medical   **7 to 10%**

Entertainment/Recreation   **3 to 5%**

Goals (Long and short term) each 5 to 10%

Miscellaneous   **3 to 5%**

Let's take a look at a sample budget. Mr. &
Mrs. Budget has a combined annual income of
$60,000. Let's calculate their annual budget.

Housing (25%)   **$15,000**

Household (15%)   **$9,000**

Transportation (10%)   **$6,000**

Clothing (5%)   **$3,000**

Insurance/Medical (7%)   **$4,200**

Entertainment/Recreation (3%) **$1,800**

Goals (10% each)   **$18,000**

Miscellaneous (3%)   **$1,800**

Take the above figures and divides each by 12
to come up with the monthly budget amounts.

Once again, feel free to copy the sample
budget form, on the next page, to do your
budget. Just remember, (1) do it NOW, and (2)
include all family members, and (3) STICK to it!

SAMPLE BUDGET

Category	Percentage *	Amount
Housing		
Household		
Transportation		
Clothing		
Insurance/medical		
Entertainment/recreation		
Goals		
Miscellaneous		
Totals		

*Use a percentage within the range that was given to you on page 27. Do your calculations from you net income. Calculate monthly budget figures by the dividing the annual figures by 12.

Once you have completed your budget, I guarantee that it will be a real eye-opener. Try to keep your budget as simple as possible. Purchase a notebook that is for your budget and your budget alone. Label the notebook-BUDGET. Do not use it to write down your grocery list. Don't allow your kids to do their homework in it. It is for your budget!

Write down *everything* you spend (even the pennies) and what purchases were made. At the end of the month, total the items according to your budget. The first month is your chance to see exactly where your money is going. Use your first budget to create a workable budget, that is, a budget that fits your income.

In order to maintain this budget you must adjust your priorities and adjust your lifestyle. If you don't make these two adjustments, you will be forced to mismanage your money. If you're like most people, you spend money on things you really don't need and things you really can't afford. Don't feel bad about this. We've all done it--remember my house slippers and matching robes.

Now is the time to correct this behavior. It takes time to develop a management behavior. Many of us are effective managers on our jobs, however, we are poor managers of our finances.

When I was the manager of an insurance agency, I made sure that everything was in order. I checked and re-checked the accounts. It was very rare that a penny slipped by me. The agents, continuously, tried to swindle commissions to support their lifestyles. If it got past me today, I would catch the mistake the next day. I was, most definitely, an effective manager.

At home, things were different. I was the ineffective manager of fifteen maxed-out credit cards, no savings, and no plans for retirement. I was a strong wind away from financial disaster!

It's essential that you "get control" of your spending. Along with controlling your money comes the matter of priorities. Setting priorities mean that you can't have everything that you want and when you want it. You must learn to determine what you NEED versus what you WANT.

If you use your budget as a planning tool, your future will be much brighter. If you ask the average self-made millionaire what is the first step to getting your finances together, the answer will be--do a budget. These self-made millionaires will tell you that they *schedule in* time each month to do their budget. They will tell you that they spend a great deal of time each month on their finances. They will tell you that they have clearly defined goals for the personal and financial aspects of their lives.

CREDIT CARDS

Make paying off your credit cards a part of your short-term goals. You have already paid enough interest, therefore, you do not need to extend credit card balances any longer than necessary. When it comes to credit cards don't curtail your spending-simply STOP! Use money from your short-term goals fund to pay off credit card debt.

Make a list of your credit cards, the current balances, and the monthly payment. Now, re-arrange the list, putting the bills with the lowest balance first. Determine how much you can add to the minimum payment of the first bill (that is $10 or more). For example, if the minimum payment is $25, and the amount you can add is $10, pay the $35 each month. Continue to pay this amount each month until the account is paid in full, even if the minimum amount goes down. Once the account is paid in full, CLOSE THE ACCOUNT.

After you have paid off the first bill, you need to allocate that monthly payment elsewhere. Take the minimum amount ($25) and start a savings account. Take the additional amount ($10) and add it to the next bill.

You need to start a savings account as soon as possible. You will need the savings in case of an emergency. If an emergency occurs, and you don't have a savings to cover it, then you will be tempted to use the credit card that you have just paid off. Even though you have just closed the account, the creditor will be more than glad to re-open it for you. And this will put you back in the same position.

An emergency fund is critical to your financial success. There are many minor disasters that could occur, and they seem to happen when you're least expecting them. It's a good idea to have a reserve fund to draw from in the event of an unexpected expense.

Remember, your "emergency" fund is just that- it's ONLY for emergencies. It should not be used as extra money or play money. For example, the 26 year old central air unit decides to go into retirement. The cost to replace it is $900. If you don't have a savings (emergency fund), what will you do when the temperature is 100 degrees and the humidity is 80%? You will use a credit card or open a *new* account to purchase a new central air unit. Now, you are back in debt and have defeated your purpose of getting out of debt. However, if you have your emergency fun, you can get the $900 out of the fund. The problem is solved using "cash" and not a credit card.

Let's see how Mr. & Mrs. In-Debt move to become debt-free.

Bills	Balance	Min. Pymt.
Gas Card	$500	$25
Furniture Co.	$1000	$50
Retail #1	$2000	$100
Retail #2	$2500	$100
MasterCard	$5000	$150
VISA	$10,000	$250

Mrs. In-Debt has determined that she can pay an additional $25 on the lowest bill. So, she starts to pay $50 each month. In a year's time, the balance is $0. (A year seems like a long time, and it is a long time. Just remember, it takes longer it get out of debt than it does to get in debt.) Next, she calls the company and closes the account. Now, she has an extra $50. She takes $25 (the minimum payment) and starts a savings account. She applies the other $25 to the next bill.

I must stop here to say that not many banks will let you open an account with $25. So, you will need to hold the money until you have enough to open the account. If you can not trust yourself, have someone whom you can trust to hold the money for you. This is not the time to pretend like you can trust yourself, if you know that you will spend the money. Don't risk your financial freedom for $25! By the way, there is no such thing as "hiding it from yourself". *You* hid it, so *yourself* knows where it is located. Put the money in trusting hands.

Back to Mrs. In-Debt-she takes the extra $25 and applies it to the furniture bill. A year has past (while we were paying the gas card bill), so the balance is about $700 (down from $1000). She begins to pay $75 each month (the $50 payment plus the $25 extra payment). In approximately nine months, this balance is paid in full. Two down and four more to go!

Mr. In-Debt suggests that they take the $75

and go out to dinner. That's a great ideal to celebrate the accomplishments and sacrifices that you have made toward your financial goals. However, the next month, get back on track.

In the past nine months, while paying off the furniture bill, Mr. & Mrs. In-Debt has saved $225. Now that the furniture bill has been paid in full, they will have an additional $75. So, Mrs. In-Debt will be adding an additional $25 to the savings, making the monthly deposit $50, and adding $50 to the Retail #1 bill, making the monthly payment $150.

Mr. & Mrs. In-Debt continues until their credit card bills are paid in full. By the time the final bill is paid, they are saving $125 each month, up from $25. They, also, have $550 in extra cash. They can pay this amount as extra payments for the car or house, or they can fund their investment accounts. The point being- now, they have choices. Choices are a sure sign of freedom, and freedom means joy!

Guess what? Mr. & Mrs. In-Debt has changed their name to Mr. & Mrs. Debt-Free. Next month, they are planning a debt-free vacation (the best kind). This is the first vacation that they have ever had, that they didn't have to worry about how they were going to pay for it.

The trip is paid in full before they leave, and their spending will be in the form of traveler's checks, and not credit cards.

I remember the first month that I became debt-free. It was a strange, but great feeling. Each time I got paid, I was looking for a bill to pay. There were no bills! When the utility bills came in, I would immediately write a check and mail them. I did this so that I could write a check. I use to go through a box of checks in three months! Now, a box of checks last me over a year.

Make "pay as you go" your family name, and wear it proud. Be proud of the fact that you have discipline and live debt-free. The self-esteem of living debt-free is more psychologically satisfying than keeping up with the deeply in-debt Jones. Some of the Jones you are trying to keep up with are not in debt. When people ask you (as they ask me), how can you *afford* to do this or that. Tell them, " I can afford to do it, because I am *debt-free.*"

Do what you can with what you have, where you are.   *Theodore Roosevelt*

2

CLOTHING

I know that there are many people who must have the lastest fashion as soon as it appears in the store's window. There are few people who can *afford* to pay full price for clothes. Most of the people I have talked to who pay full price for their clothes are heading to or deep into a financial crisis. This kind of spending will destroy your financial goals.

You must always be aware of how much things cost. That way, when you see a "sale" sign, you will know whether or not it is actually a "sale". For example, you see a purse that you are thinking of purchasing for $50. You put the purse back and decide to wait for a sale. You, later, see an ad showing your purse and others "on sale" 2 for $100. Have you actually saved any money? No, but if you are not aware of the price, you will think that it is a "sale".

If you are not aware of pricing, what do you do? Armed with the sales paper, you head to the store. You think-what a deal! So, you buy two purses for the $100. What happens next? You tell a friend about the deal you got, only to find out that it wasn't a deal. Your friend got her purse for $37.50 ($50 minus 25% discount) from a "sale" the week before. If you have ever worked retail, then you know that the price of merchandise goes down one week, then up the next week, so be aware of pricing.

Many people claim to be *bargain shoppers*, however, they lose the value of the bargain by using credit cards. To purchase a $100 blouse for $25 is a bargain, if you pay cash. To purchase the same blouse with a credit card that you pay the balance off each month, still makes it a bargain. However, to purchase the same blouse with a credit card that maintains a monthly balance and receives a minimum monthly payment, doesn't make the blouse a bargain. Depending on your balance, within months, your $25 bargain can cost you $100 (the original price). In essence, you have not saved.

Most of the time, I am wearing designer clothing. I love designer clothing. I love the uniqueness of the various lines by the various designers. Throughout my life, I have had goals for myself. Had I allowed myself to continue paying designer prices for designer clothing, I would not have been able to achieve many of my goals. I had to get control of my spending and free up money to invest in my goals.

The majority of the designer outfits that I have were purchased at 50% to 75% off of the original price. I purchase my outfits from the *clearance racks.* This is my first and last stop in a store. A " sale" rack does not draw me. But a "clearance" rack draws me like a powerful magnet. People greet me with "How much did you pay for that?" The prices I pay for clothing are unbelievable, and I just love it!

If you *really* went through your closet, you will find at least five items that still have price tags on them. Finding five tagged items in your closet means that you don't have an **immediate** need for clothing. So, take this time to examine your clothing budget amount and curtail your spending to fit your budget.

When allocating a percentage to your clothing budget, be reasonable. If your job requires you to wear a uniform, such as a nurse, don't expect your clothing budget to be the same as someone working in corporate america. At the same, Mr. & Mrs. Corporate USA, don't try to make your budget the same as Oprah. Remember, Oprah can *afford* the black belt that she has in shopping. However, you will probably use the higher percentage.

Sit down with your entire family when making your budget. Establish an amount in your budget for clothing. Let each child know *exactly* how much he will be allotted for clothing annually. Keep your child abreast of how much he has spent and the remaining balance. *Stick to your budget!*

With careful shopping, you can cut your old spending habits in half. The $3000 that you spent last year, can be $1500 this year. Take the $1500 that you saved and invest it.

Discount stores, outlet stores, and warehouses don't always mean an instant bargain. I have gone to many of these stores and found the prices only a few pennies cheaper than the regular stores. So, don't be fooled by the title. On many occasions, I didn't find a *real bargain* until I reached my "trusty" clearance rack.

Many of the clothes I have are purchased at

the end of the season. In the clothing industry, the seasons end before the calendar season. Therefore, I am able to wear my clothes and not have to hold them until the next year.

Shopping with a teenager can be a health hazard along with a financial disaster. This is another reason why adults should have their spending habits in control. You can't shop like it is the last time you will be able to go to a store and expect your children not to react the same way. Parents spend in excess of $3000 a year per child on designer clothing.

How many baby clothes have you seen that were worn out? Babies grow at such a fast rate, until they don't have a chance to wear each outfit more than five times. We continue to spend $50 to $75 (or more) for each designer items because it's "cute". Many times, baby clothes are passed on to 3 or 4 kids before they are actually worn out. I'm not saying that your child should not wear designer clothes. Like myself, my son has on designer clothing, almost daily. He was a "designer baby", too. However, $50 included a designer shirt, designer pants, and designer shoes. Now, that he is older, $50 won't include the shoes. You can purchase the "best" for "less".

It wouldn't be a chapter about clothing, if I

didn't mention my beloved "shoes". Those who know me understand- for I am truly a shoe lover, and I believe the shoes make the outfit.

Over the past ten years, the prices of shoes have been reduced greatly. There was a time when a quality pair of shoes cost $100 or more. As of late, I have found some quality and classy shoes for less than $50. It is my rule to buy a good shoe at a bargain price. I do not advocate buying poor quality shoes. Rather than buying a poor quality shoe, and risk damaging my feet, I will wait for a sale on a quality built shoe.

The majority of the shoes that I purchase are very conservative. That means that they do not go out of style overnight. I rarely purchase "fashion" shoes. Fashion shoes that you purchase this year are no longer in style the next year. Whether you buy conservative or fashion shoes, choose quality first.

For a summary on clothing:

- Establish a clothing budget with your family

- Shop the clearance racks

- Purchase designer clothing for less

- Buy clothes at the end of the season

- Make sure a "sale" is actually a "sale"
- Buy quality shoes

Some of my favorites places to shop:

Clothing--T. J. Maxx and Marshalls

Shoes--Nordstrom Rack and Spiegel Outlet

Coat/Outerwear--Burlington Coat Factory

Household Items--Wal-Mart and Target

Always be a first-rate version of yourself,
instead of a second-rate version of somebody
else.   *Judy Garland*

3

AUTOMOBILE

The question that I can not answer is-why does it take *all day* to buy a car? For this reason, it is the one purchase that I hate to make.

When you go in to purchase a car, you say to the salesman, "Hi my name is Lisa". He disappears for 15 to 20 minutes to clear *your name* with the sales manager. You ask for change for the vending machine. The salesman disappears, again, to get clearance from the finance manager. The purpose of the car salesman must be to walk the lot in the freezing and boiling hot temperatures. Once inside, he has no power (except walking power). So, give the power to yourself.

When you go to purchase an automobile, you have a **team** (salesman, sales manager, and finance manager) working against you. Therefore, you need to arm yourself with a **team.**

First, you need to determine what a car means to you. Is it a status symbol, or is it a means of transportation? This chapter is for "transportation seekers" only. It is too costly to purchase a status symbol car. Status seekers are driven by how much they pay for a car. The higher the price, the more complete they feel.

Second, get on the Internet and do some research on the car that your are thinking about purchasing. Doing your research will give you a reasonable price range for the car. You can go to www.edmunds.com and www.kbb.com to look up the actual dealer cost on the base vehicle and the options that you are considering. Calculate the two cost from both websites, as they may be slightly different. Take this info with you to the dealership for negotiation.

Next, determine whether or not the insurance on the model that you have selected is reasonable. So many people go in to purchase a car without considering the cost of the insurance. Many times, the monthly payments for the insurance is the same (or more) than the monthly payment on the car.

The next step is to get **pre-qualified** for a car loan. Credit union rates are usually cheaper than a bank or finance company. If you qualify for the low, low dealer advertised rates, by all means take advantage of them.

Don't forget budgeting! Go back to your budget and see how much of a car payment you can afford. If the monthly payment of the car you plan to purchase extends beyond your budget, you should choose another car or a cheaper model. If the cheapest of a cheap car is beyond your budget, you should consider a car without a car payment.

If your budget allows for a $570 payment and your car payment is $320, use the $250 difference to pay the car off early. In other words, send in a $250 principal payment along with the $320 monthly payment. If you have a low interest rate, such as 0.9% or 1.9%, it will not be beneficial to pay off the loan early. It will be best to invest the $250.

NEW CAR

For the goodness of your money, let's purchase a new car using maximum saving.

Now that you have been pre-qualified for your car loan, go out and purchase a newspaper. Look for ads for the vehicle that you are considering.

Dealers will advertise a car a few hundred dollars over the base price to pull customers into the dealership. These cars don't have a lot of added options. If you are a transportation seeker, such as myself, all the added options are not important. When you find that ad for the car you are looking for, head to the dealership (don't forget your newspaper and pre-approval).

It is best to go to the dealership when it is closed and find the car yourself, using the sticker number given in the ad. Go back to the dealership when it is open and test drive a car like the one you are thinking about buying. If you find that this is the car for you, then tell the salesman you want to look at some of the other cars and pick the one in the ad. Of course, he will try to talk you out of the car, because it is a cheaper one. When inside the dealership, show him the ad, and tell him this is the price you will pay. Don't try to negotiate the price down any lower, for the dealership has already done that for you, in the ad. Just take the deal and drive away happy.

In 1999, I purchased my new car for $3500 less than the sticker price by buying the car in the ad. Plus, I had a pre-qualified loan for 4 years at 2.9% interest.   What a deal!

Another thing I did was calculate the payment on the Internet at www.cars.com. This proved to be *very important.* Even though the dealership showed 2.9% interest on the papers, they had calculated a higher interest rate. The higher rate resulted in a $100 increase for each monthly payment. I showed them my calculations, and the payments were reduced-a $4800 scam!

My total saving on this deal was over $15,000 (cost of the car, interest, the scam, and the extended warranty). Talk about a calculated blessing-my saving was more than the cost of the car!

Again, save yourself hundreds of dollars by NOT buying your extended warranty and car insurance from the dealership. Do a search on the Internet and compare. I saved $1150 on the extended warranty.

Having car alarms, striping, etc. done at the

dealership is costly. Save your money and go to a company that specializes in those areas.

USED CAR

Any car, new or used, has the potential to be a lemon. However, there are steps you can take to avoid thousands of dollars in losses when buying a used car.

As with a new car, do an Internet search on the vehicle you are thinking about buying to determine a reasonable price. While on the Internet, check the cost of insurance for the car. If the cost of the car and the cost of the insurance is in close proximity, it will be more cost efficient to purchase liability insurance only.

Get a pre-approved loan before you go to purchase the car. If possible, try *not* to finance a used car. The interest rates on a used car tend to be much higher than the interest rates on a new car. If you must finance the car, watch for deals at your bank and/or credit union. Both institutions will be less than the dealership.

Once you have found your car, write down the VIN # and tell the salesman you will be back. If the car you are purchasing is a 1982 or newer, you can go to www.carfax.com and get a Vehicle History Report. The Vehicle History Report will help you to determine if the used car you are buying has been:

- In an accident (or many accidents)

- Totaled by an insurance company

- In a flood or other natural disasters

- The number of owners and the date they bought the car

- Whether or not the car was leased, a rental car, or a fleet car

- Stolen and/or rebuilt

- When the dealer took delivery and the odometer reading

There is a small fee for the report, but it is nothing compared to the headaches you can have for **not** doing the report. You can, also, use the report to negotiate a purchase price. This report is of utmost importance to a used car buyer. Pay the money and run the full report. You will be glad you did.

If you have a Sam's Club Membership, you can get a Vehicle History Report <u>free</u>. If you have an Elite Membership, you can get up to 5 Vehicle History Reports <u>free</u>.

The car selling team can't be trusted, so arm yourself with your buying team. Here is your car buying team:

1. Do an Internet search on the car

2. Check the cost of the insurance

3. Get a pre-approved loan

4. Look for the vehicle in the newspaper

5. Calculate your payment, if you will be using the dealer's financing

6. Drive away with a deal

When one door shuts, another opens.

Proverbs

4

HOUSING

One of the most expensive purchases you will make in your lifetime is the purchase of a home. Since it is a major purchase, it is something that you should plan for in advance.

To begin, you should get a copy of your credit report from all three major credit bureaus-- Equifax, Experian, and TransUnion. It is very important that you obtain all three reports, for each company may have different information. Read all of the reports and make sure that the credit reports are correct. If there are any errors, take the necessary steps to correct them. Once you have all corrected reports, you are ready to take the next step.

Next, determine how much you can *afford* to pay based on what you are paying for housing now. Are you paying your rent or mortgage with ease, or are you struggling to meet the payment each month? To make a financially sound decision, use the percentage (25% to 30%) given in Chapter 1.

With this amount in mind, take your credit report and go into a mortgage company to be pre-qualified. It is important to take these steps promptly. Going into a mortgage company with a six month old credit report will not work. Credit reports change every three months. If your credit reports are old, the loan officer will have to order new ones.

The loan officer will tell you the maximum loan amount that you qualify for to buy your new home. If your maximum amount is $175,000 that doesn't mean that you must buy a $175,000 house. Consider the payment on a $175,000 house versus the budget payment amount that you calculated. The last thing you want to be is "house broke". If a $125,000 house is more comfortable for you, then, that is what you should be buying.

Beware of mortgage brokers! A mortgage

broker finds mortgages for homebuyers. You don't need a mortgage broker to find a mortgage for you.

A mortgage broker's main goal is profit. They must be paid for their services, so they charge you. Their fees are usually tacked into the closing cost. The interest rates you will be quoted are a lot higher than that of a mortgage company.

In one case, a buyer paid over $9000 to purchase a $70,000 house. Had the buyer gone directly to a mortgage company or a bank, he would have paid approximately $3500.

Your next step is to choose a real estate agent. In larger cities, there will be thousands and your picking will be tough. Therefore, ask for some recommendations from family and friends.

Real estate agents appreciate your loyalty to them for their time and effort, however, if you don't feel comfortable with the agent--try another one. This is a major purchase, and you need to feel that the agent is working for **you.** If you are considering new construction, **never** negotiate with the builder directly. Do your negotiations through a buyer's agent or a real estate attorney.

In all real estate transactions, use a real estate attorney. If you don't know one, once again, ask family or friends for referrals. Many times, the real estate agent can give you the names of several attorneys. Don't bother calling your personal injury attorney to negotiate a real estate deal for you.

Over the years, I have seen buyers struggle to get out of bad deals. Many have lost lots of money and others had to pay lots of money to resolve problems. Other attorneys usually don't have a clue as to what is needed to clear up real estate matters.

A real estate attorney will know how to negotiate lower taxes for your new home. A real estate attorney will know the real estate language and can write a contract that's in your favor. A real estate attorney will be able to resolve title problems quickly and efficiently. Problems in real estate can be very expensive and hard to resolve. That is why, it is wise to hire qualified professionals.

Now that you have your loan officer, real estate agent, and real estate attorney, let's find your house.

In looking for a house, some of the factors you should consider are the schools, your commute to and from work, environmental hazards, and what's currently happening in the community itself. Are there a lot of "for sale" signs? Are there a lot of board-ups or vacant homes? Are there a lot of turnovers in the commercial area? Are there new communities being built? Is there a lot of commercial construction going on? All of these factors play into the future of the community and the future value of your house.

Make your offer to purchase in writing. Many sellers are offended by verbal offers, because they feel that you are trying to swindle them out of their property. Plus, they are less likely to accept your offer when you do put it in writing.

Additionally, don't try to flatter the seller with a low "cash" offer. Seller are aware that there are very few cash buyers, and don't buy into the gimmick.

When writing up your offer with your agent (or real estate attorney), don't assume that the seller won't accept your offer. There is always a negotiation cushion in the asking price--use it. The worst thing that can happen is your offer is rejected.

A home inspection is a must have for a used home. There can be problems that the sellers are aware of and fail to disclose. There can, also, be problems that the sellers don't know exist. It is good and worthwhile for you to protect yourself. Your real estate agent should be able to give you a list of home inspectors, or contact the American Society of Home Inspectors (ASHI).

A lot of people assume that new construction homes don't need a home inspection. It doesn't matter whether or not the house is new or used, a home inspection is a necessity. Don't rely on city or county building inspectors to inspect *your* house. They are paid to look out for the city's or county's interest. Pay someone to look out for your interest, because builders do make mistakes. Builders will cover up their mistakes, because many mistakes are too costly to correct.

Appliances are usually optional in new construction homes. If the appliances are optional, opt-not to purchase them with the house. If you do, the appliances will be financed with the purchase price of the house over the 30 years. Over 30 years, you will pay more than 5 times the original price of the appliances.

If you are buying your first home, it is my recommendation that you curtail your spending habits for at least a year. New homeowners are so excited about their new home that they go out and buy new carpeting, new custom drapes and blinds, a house full of new furniture, new appliances, and a new car to park in the driveway. These new bills, coupled with the mortgage payments, could force you into foreclosure. To keep yourself out of this position, put off buying any big ticket items that you don't need right away.

The mortgage is your biggest expense in purchasing a home. This is the area where you should look to cut your costs. The average mortgage is 30 years. You can save thousands of dollars by paying your mortgage off early.

How do you do this? Each month send in an extra payment. This payment is to be applied to your *principal only.* The principal is the amount of the loan before the interest is added. The more you send in, the faster your mortgage will be paid off.

If you can't afford extra payments now, consider bi-weekly payments. You can shorten your years on your mortgage and save on the interest. Contact your bank or mortgage company before you start making bi-weekly payments.

I have heard people say that they don't want to pay their mortgage off early-they need it for a "write-off" on their taxes. Consider the following example before you make that decision.

A $100,000 mortgage with a fixed interest rate of 8% for 30 years will cost you $255,352. Let's assume you consistently made extra principal payments, saving 50% of the interest ($77,676). Can you honestly say that you will receive over $77,000 in deductions from the IRS? I don't think so! Take the deductions for each year that you have the mortgage, but make it a goal to pay the mortgage off early. The $77,000 invested is your money being good to you!

Being *consistent* with your principal payments is very important. You will take years off of your mortgage and save thousands.

HOUSEHOLD ITEMS

A year has passed, and you should be adjusted (financially) to the mortgage payment and the expenses of the new house. Let's consider buying furnishings for the house. The best advice I can give you is the "clearance" room.

In the clearance room, you will find items marked down 60% to 80% off of the original price. Many of the items are missing pieces or have been slightly damaged.

When shopping for furniture, I don't stop until I reach the clearance room. I have a friend that purchased a $1000 leather sofa for $250, because of a tear in the back. She bought a leather repair kit and fixed the tear, so that it would not get any bigger. The sofa was placed against the wall, and no one ever knew. One year, I furnished two bedrooms and the living room for $2500.

Sam's Club doesn't have the usual clearance racks, but they do have clearance items. To locate the clearance items, look for price tags with prices that end with 91 cents. I found a CD player that stores 51 CD s for $159.91. On another shopping trip, I purchased a Hewlett-Packard notebook for $890.91. As a matter of fact, it is the same notebook that I used to type this book. When I checked for the same notebook in a leading electronic store, the price was $1569-on sale. What a bargain!

If you do your planning and budgeting, you will

be able to live in your house and enjoy it. You will not be debt ridden. You will be able to take a debt-free vacation and fund your children's college fund. You will not be "house broke". Planning makes your money be good to you.

Plan for the future, because that's where you are going to spend the rest of your life.

Mark Twain

5

INSURANCE

The purpose of insurance is to act as a safety net; as a protection against what might happen. Most insurance is sold on the basis of fear: The fear of what might happen and to whom it might happen.

Insurance can be divided into five different categories: auto, life, health, homeowners, and other insurances. Let's take a look at each one.

Automobile Insurance

Automobile insurance can be very costly. Your credit score, driving record, and claim record can affect your insurance rates. They can, also, determine whether or not an insurance company will accept you as a risk.

Each state has a minimum amount of liability coverage that is required. You should consider this amount, only if, you have little to no assets. The more assets you have, the more coverage you should consider.

On the comprehensive and collision portion of your insurance, a higher deductible decreases the cost of your insurance. Selecting a $500 or $1000 deductible will reduce your insurance rate.

If you have an older car, compare the value of the auto to the cost of full coverage. If the cost of the insurance and the value of the car are close, you should consider dropping the comprehensive and collision coverage. For example, if the value of the car is $2500 and the cost of the insurance is $2000, it would be wise not to buy full coverage insurance.

Ask your insurance agent about multiple car discounts, discounts for alarms/theft devices, or multiple policy discounts. The discounts are not large amounts, but every little bit adds to your wealth.

LIFE INSURANCE

There are so many life insurance policies available to you. There are life insurance policies that cover just about every stage of your life. Don't worry about trying to understand them all, because most of them you won't need.

The main purpose of life insurance is to protect your family and/or loved ones from financial disaster when you die. The amount of life insurance you will need will vary from family to family. You should purchase an amount that will enable your family to live basically the same lifestyle they had before your death.

A simple term insurance policy is usually all you will need. A term policy is actually that, a policy for a certain amount of time--1 yr., 10 yrs., 20 yrs., a lifetime. Buying a term policy will enable you to afford more coverage for the best possible price. This is actual insurance and does not include investment plans or hidden charges. You can save up to 80% of the cost of universal life insurance. Take the difference and invest it yourself.

Unless your child is a financial asset to your family, do not buy insurance on children. Invest the money into a college fund for your children.

HEALTH INSURANCE

Hopefully, you have your health insurance coverage through your job. Health insurance for a family is very costly. Group plans, such as through your job, can reduce the cost considerably.

If you have to purchase your own health insurance, there are a few things that you need to know. First, if you are not in the best of health, you will be charged exorbitant rates. Good health equals good rates.

A study at the University of Michigan showed that wealthier people enjoy better health, fitness, and quality of life as they age, on average. This is another reason to become debt-free. The stresses of everyday life along with mounting bills will create and add to health issues. By eliminating your money problems, you will have more time to enjoy life.

Striking a balance between health maintenance and wealth building should not be put off any longer. Plan now to schedule in time for rest, fun, exercise, proper nutrition, and regular dental and medical checkups.

Unfortunately, many individuals ignore their health while they focus on wealth building. It is very easy to do when you are faced with the demands of a growing business. This is an area that I, recently, had to get control of in my life. I would take the vacations (fun), however, I neglected the other areas. Now, I'm taking the time to exercise and read books about proper nutrition. I, even, take time to take in my surroundings.

To ease the cost of health insurance, consider opening a Medical Savings Account (MSA). A MSA is a combination plan that includes a health insurance policy with a very high deductible and a tax-advantaged savings account. The deductible is usually $2500, but the premium is very low. It is useless for minor medical expenses because of the $2500 yearly deductible. The money you don't pay in high premiums goes into a savings account, free of income tax. When you have medical expenses, you draw money from your MSA account until you meet the deductible. After that, the MSA health insurance policy takes over. The policy protects you, if you have a serious illness or injury.

Medical bills can be a death sentence for a family finances. In some cases, it is actually a death sentence.

HOMEOWNERS INSURANCE

Replacement cost is a valuable asset of the homeowners insurance policy. Replacement cost will pay to replace your belongings, rather than give the depreciated value. Once again, the higher deductible constitutes a lower premium. If you are happy with your auto insurance carrier, consider placing your homeowners insurance with them and request a multi-policy discount.

It's helpful to make a video or take pictures of everything in every room of your house. When you are done, store the video or photos in a fire proof safe or safe deposit box. DO NOT STORE THEM IN YOUR HOUSE! If there is a fire, a melted tape or burned album won't do you any good. The purpose of the video and photos is to help you substantiate your insurance claim in the case of theft or fire.

Coverage on your possessions are very

important. You don't want to skimp on the amount of the coverage. However, you can request a higher deductible to reduce your premiums. Make sure the higher deductible is something that you can afford to pay should a claim arises.

Mortgage and credit life insurance are a waste of money. A substitute for mortgage insurance is a term policy. Buy a term insurance policy for an amount that covers the balance of your mortgage.

Never leave that till tomorrow which you can do today.   *Benjamin Franklin*

6

INVESTMENTS

Is your goal to become financially independent? Are you willing to make the necessary changes in your life and lifestyle to reach that goal? Do you believe that you deserve millionaire status? If you answered "yes" to all of the above questions, then you must agree that you are willing to make the necessary changes to reach these goals.

If you apply the ideas and suggestions in this book, then you will have funds available for investments. If you are serious about building financial freedom for yourself and your family, then you must get control of your finances.

And you must do it NOW!

Your first investment should be a savings account. Remember, you should start saving as soon as you pay off your first bill. After you have paid off your debts, you will be ready to consider other investments.

Find a bank that has a low minimum deposit amount that you can afford. Open a savings account and begin to save. It is the "pay yourself first" plan. As you plan your budget, allocate 10% of your net pay for savings (emergency fund). As you become debt-free, plan 10% of your net pay to go to short-term savings **and** 10% to long-term savings.

Another goal should be to diversify your investments. You should spread your investment fund among dissimilar assets. This way, if one asset starts to lose value, another asset will offset the losses.

There are risks involved in investing. The more risk, the higher the return. If you can't afford to lose any of your investment, choose investments that are less riskier. Below are the risk factors for the various investments.

Lesser Risk

U. S. Treasury Bills

U. S. Treasury Bonds

Federal Agency Bonds

Moderate Risk

U. S. Corporate Bonds

Foreign Corporate Bonds

Greater Risk

Blue Chip Common Stocks

Common Stocks

Real Estate

Coins and Stamps

Futures

Many corporations sponsor plans that permit shareholders to choose to have their dividends automatically reinvested in additional shares of stocks. The plans are called *dividend reinvestment plans(DRIPs)*. DRIPs allow you to increase the number of shares you own, by reinvesting the dividends. For as little as $50, you can get started in a DRIP plan. This is a convenient and inexpensive way to start and build your stock portfolio. Most reinvestment plans permit you to contribute additional money to purchase more shares of stock.

If you are a beginner and want to learn more about investing in the stock market, I suggest that you join an investment club. An investment club is an excellent opportunity to learn about investing in the stock market.

As Coach of the Millennium Millionaires Youth Model Investment Club and a Director of the Chicago South Chapter of NAIC, I learned a great deal about investing in the stock market. I had the opportunity to interact with many knowledgeable investors. It, also, afforded me the opportunity the meet the "investment genius" Warren Buffett.

As part of your monthly schedule, be sure to attend investment seminars or investor fairs, such as those given by NAIC. Go to their website at www.better-investing.org to view a list of scheduled events in your area.

Educate yourself by reading financial literature. Some books and magazines are written by financial planner and are very complicated to understand. There are many publications that are not as complicated. NAIC in conjunction with South-Western Publishing Co. has published an excellent textbook-*Investing In Your Future.* Even though the textbook was designed for high school students, I have recommended it to many beginning investors. Many beginning investors have reported that the book has helped them greatly, especially with the terminology. You can purchase the book from NAIC's website, or your local chapter.

If you are unaware of an investment club that you can join, again, attending seminars, investor fairs, workshops, and your local NAIC chapter meeting can be a starting point for finding potential investment clubs. If you find a group of people seeking to join an investment club, get together with them and start your own club. Don't worry about being new to the game, because NAIC has books, tapes, classes, seminars, and investor fairs, whereby, you can learn everything you need to know to run an effective investment club. There is no charge for your local NAIC chapter to help you in getting your investment club started.

You should have money invested in as many investment vehicles as possible. Before you invest your money in any of these vehicles, please educate yourself about them. Find out as much as possible about each vehicle before committing your money. Definitely make sure that you know the risks involved before you invest your money.

So, start saving NOW! Pay yourself first. Reinvest all of your earnings. Don't be a "noise investor". Be patient. Make educated investment decisions and watch you money grow!

We should not let our fears hold us back from pursuing our hopes.   *John F. Kennedy*

7

TRAVEL

I LOVE TO TRAVEL! I enjoy seeing other parts of this country and far away places. It is truly amazing how different places are within the United States. There is a difference in the culture and the scenery from the South to the North and the East to the West. The mountains, hills, flatland, valleys, cities, small towns, and the country are all wonderful discoveries. I have seen the muddy waters of the mighty Mississippi River and the peaceful, aqua waters of exotic islands. And I want to see more!

It is my goal to travel to all fifty states and as

many foreign countries as possible. I know this will be costly, so I had to learn how to cut the cost of travel.

My major source of discount for travel is the Internet. I am registered with Expedia, Travelocity, Yahoo, and Orbitz to receive newsletters of their travel deals via email. There are other travel sites that I visit whenever I am looking to travel, however, I chose to only register at these sites. A new kid on the block is www.QIXO.com. This website compares the prices of dozens of travel websites, including the sites mentioned above. I have found the best deals on these five sites. I am, also, registered with many of the airlines. This way, travel deals are in front of me, almost on a daily basis.

It is good to make travel plans based on the travel deals you get from the newsletters. This makes travel more exciting, because you never know where you are going on your next vacation, until you come across the deal. Once you use this book to become debt-free, you can use those sick days or comp time to go to some of those places.

To get the best discounts, you don't always have to leave at 2 a.m., or stay in a second-rate hotel, or fly stand-by. Many major hotels have package deals with the airlines.

When making travel arrangements, you a credit card (not a debit card). It is easier to resolve any conflicts or problems that may arise when you use a credit card. The debit card does not have the same guarantee (or someone you can talk to) as with a credit card. In the case of hotels and rental car companies, they will tie-up a large sum of your travel money that's available in your debit card account. If you can, put up a cash deposit instead of letting them swipe your credit card for incidentals. If your room is paid for before you leave home, they can still tie-up amounts as large as $500 on your account, for incidentals. These amounts can be held up for several days *after* your vacation is over.

Keep all of your receipts from your vacation for at least three months after the vacation. I've had several people tell me that they have received charges on their credit cards, several months later, for bills that were paid for with cash. An imprint was made of their credit card, and the cashier, in error, charged it to their account instead of posting the transaction paid in cash. If you are traveling to a foreign country, hold onto your receipts even longer. Many times, you won't see the first charge on your account until a month or two later.

This next tip is to relieve mental anguish at the airport. If your flight has been cancelled, rather than stand in long lines with hundreds of angry and frustrated customers, use your cell phone or a pay phone to call airline reservation to rebook yourself on another flight. If you wait in line, the seats may be gone by the time you reach the counter. Plus, you don't want to be around all of the negative energy. It tends to drain you, and you are on vacation.

If you are not in a hurry to start your vacation, take advantage of the airlines' overbooking of flights. It is a super deal! When you arrive at the airport, and see a long line wrapping for miles at the gate, go directly to the counter and volunteer to give up your seat. If you are picked to give up your seat, not only will the airline book you on the next flight (either with their airline or another airline), but they will give you a travel voucher. The travel vouchers are usually between $200 and $800 for **free** travel (Due to September 11, some airlines have reduced this amount).

If you are traveling to a foreign country, you should leave a copy of your itinerary with family or friends at home. As a precaution, you should make 2 copies of your passport identification page. Leave a copy at home with friends or relatives. Carry the other with you (separate from your passport). The copy will facilitate replacement if your passport is lost or stolen.

Since the airlines are notorious for lost luggage, I use carry-on luggage *only.* I have the carry-on luggage with the wheels for all of the walking that you have to do in the airports. Make sure when you purchase your carry-on luggage, that it doesn't exceed the carry-on size limit (22 inches). As a rule, if I can't carry it on, I don't take it with me. For longer trips, I take advantage of laundry facilities. Laundry services at hotels are expensive, but it is cheaper than having to buy *all* new clothes, because the airline lost your luggage.

If you are not taking debt-free vacations, then you *should be* taking them. Make this one of your goals when your bills are paid off. Schedule debt-free vacations and discover the world.

I travel not to go anywhere, but to go. I travel for travel's sake. The great affair is to move.

Robert Louis Stevenson

8

GIVING

One of the most important lessons in life is giving. Giving is a universal law that directs paths in your life. Giving is the act of willingly parting with something in order that it may be used to benefit others.

A misconception about giving is that it takes the form of money. Giving of your time is just as important as and valuable as giving your money, because *time is money*.

Over the years, I have given both, time and money. In 1999, I was honored for my volunteer work with the prestigious Thomas Jefferson Award (a Nobel Prize for community and public service leaders started by Jacqueline Kennedy-Onassis and U. S. Senator Robert Taft Jr.). I serve on several Boards of non-profit organizations. My involvement with the Chicago South Chapter of NAIC is on a volunteer basis. In my budget, I designate 10% for giving. In my church, I am a tither, and I do believe in tithing. Between my finances and my time, I can say that I give around 25% monthly in time and money. If giving is not something you do on a regular basis, then you will probably find it hard to do, especially if you are burden with debt.

I don't believe in taking money from your monthly bills to give. Pay off your debts first. As you work on making yourself debt-free, consider giving your time. Make a list of several things that you can do to help someone else. Make a list of several causes that you would like to be involved in helping. Look over both lists and decide which one you could better service. Make a commitment NOW to volunteer one day out of the month for this cause. You will begin to see a change in your life. Giving is a life-changing experience.

Giving is not something that just happens. You have to plan for it. You have to budget for it. You must purpose in your heart to be a giver.

My purpose for writing this chapter is not to tell you how or how much you should give, but to emphasize the importance of giving. When you give, be it time or money, please do it unselfishly and cheerfully. Holding on to excess blocks your blessings.

The best exercise for the heart is to bend over backwards and help someone else.

Anonymous

GIFTS

Gift giving can be very expensive. If you sit down and make a list of the gifts, and the cost of the gifts that you have given over the past year, you will be surprised as to the amount of money you have spent. Between the weddings, graduations, birthdays (adults and children), baby showers, and the list could go on and on, you could easily max-out a credit card.

When creating a budget, make sure that you include gifts. Set a limit as to the amount that you plan to spend in the upcoming year on gifts. Take the list you made earlier, and see where you can cut your spending. Once you have reached your budgeted amount for the year, decline all other invitations. You don't need a reason, simply state that you will be unable to attend.

To eliminate the stress of gift buying, I usually purchase gift certificates for adults and teenagers (except for family and close friends), and McDonald's gift certificates for kids. Don't spend hours going from store to store trying to find the "perfect" gift for someone that has everything or is hard to satisfy. Buy them a gift certificate at a store that they frequent.

Over the years, I have heard people say that gift certificates are "thoughtless". That is not true. In fact, you *thought* about how much money you have been spending. You *thought* about all of the gifts you got over the years that you didn't want (wishing someone had given you a gift certificate). You *thought* about how much stress you were under trying to find the "perfect" gift. And last, but not least, you *thought* about them--you bought the gift certificate, didn't you?

Personally, I am *not* offended by gift certificates. Everyone now knows (from this book) the stores that I frequent. So, a gift certificate from one of these stores will be a great gift for me. Giving should be from the heart and not the pocket.

Unthankfulness is theft.   *Martin Luther*

9

KIDS

In this modern marketing society, children are a growing major consumer force. They spend over $500 billion a year. It seems as though every second of our life is filled with commercials-buy this, buy that. Large corporations are directing more and more of their advertising dollars into ads that are targeted at kids.

Kids have a never ending desire to belong or to fit. Not having the "latest" styles make them feel like social misfits. Therefore, they make constant request of their parents to buy those "gotta have" jeans, those "to be like Mike" gym shoes, or that I "wanna be a star" hair-do and nails.

Many adults are working two and three jobs just to accommodate their children with whatever they ask of them. This is their way of substituting quality time and much needed love. You can't make up the personal attention gap by buying them whatever they want. In fact, what you are doing is making your children poor managers of money, like yourself.

If you are working two and three jobs to make ends meet, that means that you have mismanaged your own money. Even though you can't afford to buy them every single piece of designer clothing and pay for weekly salon appointments, you feel obligated to do it, because you are doing the same for yourself. That's a bad example and let's turn it around.

First, start by giving your child an allowance. Determine the amount that you can afford to give them from *your* budget. Tell your child that the allowance must be spent wisely, and teach them how to do a budget. Remember, it is difficult to teach what you don't know. That means that you need to know how to do a budget, yourself.

Keep the child's budget simple. If not, he won't

be inclined to ever look at it again. Don't worry about percentages. It is too much like Math, and he will mentally shutdown (take it from a Math teacher). Just let him divide the allowance up among each category.

A sample budget for a kid could be as follows:

Clothing

Entertainment

Savings

Others (includes hobbies and school activities)

Clothing includes those expensive "designer clothes". If the child wants an expensive clothing item, make him save until he has enough to purchase the item. Don't give in and give him the money. Don't give in and loan him the money. *Teach him to save!* Over a period of time, you will see the need for those expensive items shrink, or they will request them as gifts.

When you take your child shopping, take this opportunity to teach him comparison shopping and discount shopping. Show him how he can purchase the top, bottom, and a pair of shoes for the same $100 he will be paying for one pair of shoe. Once again, you can't teach what you don't know or don't do. Take him to discount stores, where he can get more for his money. Teach him that the price tag does not determine the quality of the merchandise.

Entertainment is the category for the movies, skating, arcades, and sporting events. Help your child to determine how much will be allowed for this category, If it is $10 weekly, then the child must plan his activities accordingly.

Every year, my son purchases a Gold C Entertainment book to help stretch his entertainment dollars. It is a coupon book filled with 2-for-1 and 50% off discounts at restaurants, hotels, airlines, movies, sporting events, retail stores, and attractions. The cost of the book is $13.00, and the book is valid for a year. You can go to www.entertainment.com to order the latest copy for your child or call 1-800-933-2605. It is a *big* coupon book, so you will save a lot more than the cost of the book.

Teach your child to plan ahead for special holidays, his birthday (they usually don't have a problem doing this), and summer activities. If he starts saving in advance, he will have enough money to enjoy himself.

Savings is the most important part of the child's budget. Start your child at an early age. It doesn't matter whether the saving amount is 5 cents or $5. What your child will ultimately see is the growth of the money.

When my son was in Kindergarten, he started saving pennies. One day, he noticed that the pennies were "growing". It didn't matter to him how many pennies were in the bank. The dollar amount of the pennies didn't matter to him. The only thing that mattered to him was the pennies "growing". When the pennies reached the top, he would tell me it was time to go to the "big bank".

For older kids, teach them to save for their "big ticket" items, such as a bike, car, cheerleading uniform, class trip, prom, or graduation.

Decisions about becoming an owner of a company can start at an early age. I teach kids that there is a greater benefit in being an owner of NIKE than owning a pair of NIKE gym shoes. Once they purchase NIKE stocks and become an owner, they can buy the NIKE gym shoes. That way, they are buying the gym shoes from *themselves* and not NIKE. Plus, this is the *true* way "to be like Mike".

My son purchased Diebold stock when he

noticed the name on the machine, that took the carrier to the teller in the drive-up at the "big bank".

The Others category can include last-minute plans. This is always the last-minute social event that "everybody" will be attending. If it was not accounted for in Entertainment, this might enable him the opportunity to go ahead with his plans.

Get your child started on his budget and his saving plan. Teach him the value of a dollar early in his life, and the lesson will *grow* with the him.

Don't be afraid of growing slowly. Be afraid of standing still.   *Chinese Proverb*

10

SELF-
EMPLOYMENT

Being an entrepreneur was the biggest plus in my becoming debt-free and retiring early. At age 19, I started my first business. From a corner of my bedroom, I started Frye Insurance Agency. I owned and operated this business for 21 years. The income from this business enabled me to purchase investment properties. The income from the investment properties enabled me to pay cash for my house. The sell of the investment properties provided cash for my last business-Small Frye Academy, Inc.

Small Frye Academy, Inc. is the only elementary school in the State of Illinois for children with learning deficiencies. The success of the school led to Small Frye eAcademy, Inc. and Online Math Tutoring.

It is such a satisfying feeling in owning your own business, being your own boss, setting your own hours, being in control of your money, and reaping the benefits of your efforts.

Think about starting your own business. This is a better way to earn extra income, instead of a part-time job. However, if you are the kind of person who leaves work early, calls in sick on a regular basis, schedules an off-day for your birthday (and friends), or spending money whenever it is in your pocket, starting a business will probably not work for you. Being self-employed is not for everyone. The part-time job might be the better alternative for some. Who knows, your business venture might turn out to be an overnight success!

When most people think of starting a business, their main focus is on "setting up" shop. With no clients (or only one), they lease office space, hire a secretary, buy expensive furniture, install multiple phone lines, buy new business attire, and purchase a luxury vehicle. (I have not been able to understand the *immediate* need for a new car.) They have set-up for "success" (well actually, failure) with no way to pay for the success. This is the number one reason that most businesses fail before they begin.

Many, many years ago, I was invited to a meeting with five other insurance brokers to discuss plans for opening an insurance agency. We were to combine our "small" agencies to form a "large" agency. As they discussed the plans, I noticed that no one mentioned how they planned to generate business. No one had a marketing plan. All of the discussion was about spending-office location, furniture, expense accounts, salaries, the hiring of employees, and loads of expensive advertising (which had not been tested). When I asked who had the marketing plan, the room became silent. I was told that it would be developed as we went along, and after we were "set-up". I declined to be a part of the organization.

Obviously, there was a breakdown in their planning committee, because each of them continued their own agencies. One of the brokers even bought himself a Rolls Royce and threw a lavish party to celebrate the grand opening of his agency. It was a party to remember!!

Within three years after the initial meeting, **all** of their businesses were closed, leaving them with large amounts of debt. My home-based insurance agency survived 21 years.

Focus on making your business a success, and those other things will be added, in due time. You are the determining factor as to whether or not your business will succeed or fail. Don't waste your additional income--save it or invest it back into your business. If it fails, you will know why.

Here are some tips for starting a successful business:

- <u>Start with a product, not an office.</u> This will enable you to see if there is a need for your product.

- <u>Start small.</u> This will enable you to make mistakes, learn from the mistakes, or close the business (if necessary) without leaving you in debt.

- <u>Write a plan.</u> Write down how you plan to test the market, who you need to contact to supply you with needed materials, your advertising plan, a budget (controlling cost is very important), and determine who can benefit from your product (your selling market).

- <u>Be flexible.</u> Be willing to change as change is needed.

- <u>Build gradually.</u> Don't purchase 10,000 items to sell. Order a small quantity of merchandise, in case sales don't go as you had planned. It is easier to add a few hundred items than it is to get rid of a few hundred.

- <u>Keep good records.</u> Your financial worksheet doesn't have to look like a CPA did it. However, you do need to write down what is coming in and what is going out.

- <u>Get a separate phone line.</u> Do you know what it does for your business image when a 3 year old or a teenager with the music blasting in the background answers your business calls? Plus, your listing in the business section of your local phone book is your best form of advertising.

- <u>Develop a website.</u> Let the *world* know you are "open for business".

- <u>Read.</u> Read to get research information. Read to learn about other entrepreneurs. Read to learn, so that you can avoid as many mistakes as possible. Read to make yourself knowledgeable.

- **Be willing to share your knowledge.** In starting your business, you will need help from others. Don't forget that someone helped you, so be willing to reach out and help someone else get their business started. Believe me, there's room at the top for all of us.

Take advantage of the write-offs that are allowed through your home-based business. One benefit of having a home-based business is the federal tax advantages. The IRS allows deductions for all of your business-related expenses. If you have a home-based business, your business will pay a portion of your **legitimate** housing expenses. Use the extra cash that you, personally, save on the housing expenses to pay off bills or to invest. Don't waste it!

Everyone has something they are good at doing or enjoy doing. Decide what it is you love to do and turn it into a home-based business. Making money is easier when you are doing what you love.

The best career advice I can give to you is to figure out what you enjoy doing, do it, and get someone to pay you for doing it.   *Lisa Frye*

Look for creative ways to increase your income. Use the additional income to produce more income. Use the additional income to create another business. Use the additional income to invest. Use the additional income to become debt-free. Use the additional income to obtain your goals. Use the additional income to do good in your community. Use the additional income to retire early. Use the additional income to become financially independent. If you use the additional income to do all of these things, then you are being good to your money. The reward? Your money will be good to you!

The journey of a thousand miles must begin with a single step.   *Lao-Tze*

Congratulations! You have just made that single step to a journey of many riches. I truly hope that this book has been an inspiration to many to become debt-free and to live your dreams. *The rewards are great! I am always looking for debt-free friends, so, please email me at Lisa@LisaFrye.com and let me know how your journey began, how its coming along, and the riches you received along the way. See you at the top!*

Lisa

ACKNOWLEDGMENTS

I would like to take this opportunity to express my sincere gratitude to the wonderful people, who gave of their time to critiique and review this book. Thank you for the positive comments. They, all, meant so much to me.

Thanks to Quentin Sampson for unselfishly sharing his wealth of knowledge and words of wisdom with me, over the years.

Thanks to my family and friends for sharing your stories with me.

A special thanks goes to my oldest brother, Charles, for supporting his baby sister through the good times, bad times, and the crazy times. Thanks to you and your lovely wife for providing me with a quiet getaway to type my book.

And last, but not least, thanks to you, the reader, for caring enough about your finances to buy this book. Don't **waste** the money you used to pay for this book. Use this book, and use it again, and again, to gain the financial freedom that you so rightfully deserve, for...

THE BEST IS YET TO COME!

SUGGESTED READING

Do It: Let's Get Off Out Buts
Peter Mc Williams

Life 101
Peter McWilliams

Wealth 101: Wealth Is Much More Than Money
John Rogers & Peter Mc Williams

The Millionaire Next Door
Thomas Stanley & William Danko

How To Be Rich
J. Paul Getty

The Richest Man In Babylon
George C. Clason

The Intelligent Investor
Benjamin Graham

Printed in the United States
1382900001B/163-171

9 780972 603287